THE CLAPPER BRIDGES
OF DARTMOOR

AND SOME MYTHS AND
TALL TALES OF THE MOOR

John Stuart

ISBN 9781 898 964 919

ORCHARD PUBLICATIONS
2 Orchard Close, Chudleigh, Newton Abbot, Devon TQ13 0LR
Telephone: 01626 852714

Acknowlegements

Photography

Moorland pictures, some birds, plants and butterflies by John Stuart
Other pictures from Wikipedia free encyclopaedia

Special thanks to Chris and Graham of Virtual Hebrides for their kind invitation
to use their pictures.

THE CLAPPER BRIDGES OF DARTMOOR

People collect all sorts of things on Dartmoor and over time things can become obsessions. Out on the Moor, near Teignhead Farm I met a man (they appear out of nowhere) who was carrying a haversack full of boxes of cards, pads, stamps and a GPS device. He was letterboxing, showed me how it is done and said he'd been at it for 20 years. I thought that was an obsession but friends reminded me of my own. Then there are crosses all over the Moor, ancient settlements, some clearly seen such as the medieval village below Hound Tor, and along with them goes the study of farming methods, communications and building techniques. Mining provides huge scope for research, some long walks and not a little risk for the careless. Providing water for farms, to turn wheels at mines and mills, the many leats, dry or still running, invite interesting walks with spectacular views to be had. And on the way to see all the interesting features of the Moor, people have to cross waterways, hardly noticing the stone bridges over them and this is my personal obsession. Some ancient, some new, some of just one stone, some veritable motorways made of slabs so large and obviously heavy that the mind boggles at the effort required to position them.

So what is a clapper bridge? Well, on Dartmoor a 'clapper' is a flat stone. There are various explanations for the name, including a French one, but they are not relevant. Dartmoor being composed of granite there is plenty of stone lying around and this can be used as it is or split to produce flat pieces. This too is an interesting procedure. A clapper bridge, therefore, is one over a waterway, made of such stones, just a single slab, one placed on piers each side, or several slabs supported on mid-stream piers. All the slabs, known as imposts, and the piers are held in place only by careful placing and their own weight, no cement or other fixing being used. The collection of clapper bridges really can become an obsession. The search begins by examining the map and finding likely spots where tracks cross waterways. Nor will this be enough because there are many which seem neither to come from nor to lead anywhere. In some cases the OS have been kind enough to mark them but in at least one case a clapper is marked but has been superseded by a modern road bridge.

I have not tried to show all the clappers on the Moor. The best I can do is to suggest walking to see a selection or to follow a series such as those over a leat and above all to enjoy the delights of Dartmoor. Choose your day. A single slab over a dry ditch on a featureless hillside shrouded in mist or torrential rain is hardly an entrancing sight but if it is one of a series which simply must be followed and if it forms the foreground to a wonderful view it can make the whole day worthwhile. Most of the clappers are over leats and these can be very long – Devonport and Wheal Emma are over 10 miles long and for the most part offer only "there and back" walks and must be taken in sections. Some involve long walks, so are available only for the fit, while others can involve a lot of driving.

Along the way there are many other interesting things to see and some of these such as birds, plants and butterflies are used in spaces during this work. Reading about the Moor, you cannot fail to notice the many stories about the strange things that have happened and the people who feature in them. I have gathered some of these under the title of Myths and Tall Tales of the Moor. While the subject of the clappers needs no padding, the two are often connected and both add to the interest of Dartmoor.

The word "I" appears perhaps too much in this work but it has been a very personal search and it has taken me to all parts of the Moor. I go solo, which I am sure is unwise but for some I go too fast, for others too slow and when we get to a clapper bridge it has to be photographed. One view is never enough and I can take half an hour or more, trying the various angles, including from in the stream, waiting for the sun to come out, people to move off and animals to get into photogenic positions. By the way, if you ask "do you know the one at such and such a place?" the answer is probably yes but although I have visited about 200 there is always room for more if you find them. Like audiences, you will be pleased to hear that you are not going to see all of them. One thing before you set out; take all the necessary precautions for walking on the Moor. A few suggestions are included later.

A Dartmoor pony. Unlike on Exmoor, Dartmoor is also home to many cross-bred ponies. They multiply and there is little demand for them so they go for meat abroad. Enjoy your chorizo. They must not get used to junk food so don't feed them.

There are many ways to approach Dartmoor. The B3212 road takes you from Exeter via Dunsford and Moreton Hampstead, with oak woods on the way. The trees were mostly coppiced, having been used in the past for metal smelting. There are also "previews" of the Moor, such as the vista above, from Longdown in the autumn. The road is narrow and winding.

This, and many others, some bigger, some smaller, is what we are going up to see, and with the clapper bridges some magnificent views. With them also, some of the Myths and Tall Tales of the Moor.

Though it is not a convenient system for actually visiting clapper bridges, it makes sense to group them under the main headings of Rivers and Leats. Apart from these two principal groups there are what I call 'Outliers' – unrelated to all the others and some of these we shall see as we go along. So let us start with the ones that began my search. Getting to know the Moor after some years away and looking at the map for something interesting to look at, my eye lit on an area near Gidleigh 671884 and so we start on :

THE RIVER TEIGN

At GR 654871 is a site called Teign e Ver. There the river Teign is joined by the Walla Brook. I should say 'a' Walla Brook as there are several around the Moor. This one is very short, coming from below Hangingstone Hill 617861, where it starts so far up the hill that it almost touches the source of the East Dart on the ridge. Teign e Ver is a delightful place, with the two streams, many rocks and rowan trees making a pleasant picnic site. (Please take your litter away with you). Friends have even swum in a pool though it might be better not to show that picture.

The Teign is crossed here by two clappers, the better known one having two slabs or 'imposts' on rock foundations at the river banks and supported by a mid-stream pier. One slab has clearly been repaired and indeed the whole bridge has been rebuilt. My thanks to Dartmoor National Park Authority (hereafter just DNPA) for the picture. A few yards downstream the Teign is crossed by two slabs bound together by iron bands. Here the banks are straight and almost vertical. This is not a feat of nature but has to do with Streaming, a process of tin mining. Before it joins the Teign, the Walla Brook is crossed by a single slab bridge. Up the hill from the rivers runs the Gidleigh leat and this is also crossed by clappers. Those interested might find it fun to see how many can be found within 100 yards or so.

Cotton Grass
Eriophorum angustifolium
Actually a sedge. Thrives in marshy areas, food plant for butterfly larvae and grouse. The 'Cotton' is the long white hairs that help disperse the seeds. Once used to stuff pillows but the staple is too short to weave.

4

Teign e Ver

A few yards downstream stands a great rock called the Tolmen Stone. Thousands of years of flood water washing a stone round in a hollow has worn a hole right through it. It is said that if you go down through it, it will cure your arthritis. Not entirely true. You have to go down head first. It's about ten feet down to the rocks below, the sides are very smooth and there's nothing to hold onto. Don't even try.

My French friend tried but without success

Above, at Teign e Ver, a single slab clapper over the Walla Brook. Below, staff of DNPA repairing the large clapper in 1999.

7

This is Scorhill Tor, very close to Teign e Ver and only a few yards above the Gidleigh leat. Follow the leat beyond the tor, use the cart clapper over the leat and you come to Scorhill Circle. Originally some sixty stones, now down to thirty, of which some are lying flat, some still upright, including one of the tallest on the Moor. It can be assumed that the others have been removed for inclusion in buildings nearby. One stone lying flat shows the 'feather and tare' method of splitting rocks, the metal leaves having been left in their holes but abandoned. In days gone by women taken in adultery were taken to the circle and made to kneel before a standing stone and pray for forgiveness. Sorry about that, ladies; in these stories it's always the women who come off worse. The young men who get them into trouble never seem to have to pay up. Anyway, if her sins were forgiven the stone remained upright, but if they were too heinous it slowly collapsed upon her. They do say that a female skeleton has been found under one of the stones. And now, on stormy nights, flickering lights are seen and there is the smell of roasting flesh. After dark no horse or dog will go along the track that runs through the circle. Don't blame me; it's just what 'They' say. Knowing the tale, a Gidleigh-born lady tells me she took her little brother there and made him kneel likewise. As far as I know, he survived.

The massive cart-clapper at Teignhead farm

The easiest way to get to Teignhead is to drive to Fernworthy reservoir, drive all round to a space for a few cars, walk up through the forest, bear left at the first main junction, on up and finally down to the forest gate. That's where my friend the letter-boxer pointed me to another little clapper a short way downstream. It makes a very attractive scene. The now ruined farm is in the distance, among the trees.

Going up to Teignhead Farm, a sheep makes use of a clapper over a little tributary of the Teign that you might miss unless you see it from the stream.

This is Teignhead. The farmhouse, now ruined, is in the distant trees. The farm was established in the 1780s by Mr Rogers, as a 'newtake' from the Moor. The bridge was built in 1827, replacing an earlier one washed away by flood, to give access for vehicles. It is one of the biggest on the Moor. For the record, it has four piers, three openings, nine great slabs, 28ft long, 6ft 9ins wide. Following the track up to the farm you might miss another clapper on the way. But those stones did not get there by accident and a view from upstream confirms it.

The Skylark
Alauda Arvensis
Resident bird. Nests on the ground. Feeds on seeds and insects. The male sings in flight, his song lasting two-three minutes. Females prefer males who sing and hover longest.

MOORLAND TIPS

The Moor is a National Park. It belongs to all of us. Please make sure that your enjoyment of it doesn't spoil it for others.

* Don't start fires.
* Keep dogs under control.
* Shut gates.
* Keep to public paths across farmland.
* Leave livestock, crops and machinery alone.
* Take your litter away with you. Nobody else can collect it. A bottle will drown a small animal.
* Don't pollute waterways.
* Use proper gates and stiles to cross walls and fences.
* Don't harm animals, especially on the road. They were here before us.
* Don't feed ponies. The junk food you give them will not be here in the winter and they will starve.
* Walking beside flowing leats, don't damage the banks.

Driving on the Moor.
* Keep speed down.
* Round the next corner is an idiot who is on the wrong side of the road, half blind and can't drive. He thinks the same about you.
* Wait for animals.

Personally
* It will almost certainly rain, so take waterproofs.
* Have proper footwear with ankle support.
* Always have a map and know where you are.
* If you get 'Pixie-led' or temporarily uncertain of your position, don't be too proud to go back to where you last knew exactly where you were.
* A stick will push you uphill, keep you on a slope, steady you on the way down or over streams and rocky places. It needs to be a bit above waist high. Some use walking poles. Either may prevent falls and injury.
* Let someone know where you are going.
* Before drinking from streams, be aware that animals also use them as toilets and sometimes die in them.
* Be aware of bogs. If the ground moves under you it is time to be somewhere else.
* If not in the first flush of youth don't go off like a mad thing, take it easy till you are fit.

THE GRIMSTONE AND SORTRIDGE LEAT

This is by no means the longest leat but it is full of interest. Drawing water from the River Walkham with a head weir at 553773, it follows the course of the river till it goes through the Merrivale quarry. It is still flowing strongly, but a further leat was constructed above it to allow the development of the quarry without interfering with the water supply. In the event it proved unnecessary and was abandoned. It now runs, dry, on the north side of the B3357 road, with two clappers, one hidden by scrub growth.

The original leat follows below the road till it comes to the stream in Beckamoor Coombe, where it crosses the stream by a little aqueduct. Below that, on the west side of the leat, lies an abandoned millstone, probably intended as a grindstone in a now ruined blacksmith's workshop. When the G&S leat reaches Windy Post, where there is a stone cross, it passes under a cart-clapper and meets a division. Here is a 'Bull's eye' or 'inch stone'. This is a block of granite with an inch diameter hole drilled through. This diverts water westwards to Moor Town farm. On its way south, going round Pew/Pu Tor, further bullseyes send water to other farms. The leat was built to supply the Grimstone and Sortridge Manors. They date from the 15th C. How soon after that the leat began no-one knows but it could be extremely old. A problem arises because the G&S Manors, being at the end of the leat, and water being taken off for other farms, they were the first to suffer in time of drought. Along its course the leat is crossed by a number of clappers. There are parking bays beside the road, so a moderate walk can be had within reach.

On the north side of the road are Great, Middle and Little Staple Tors, Roos Tor and Cox Tor. A fairly energetic walk can take in all three and provide panoramic views on and off the Moor.

Snipe
Gallinago Gallinago
Nests on ground, feeds on worms and insects. Sometimes considered a game bird and shot. When disturbed flies off in zig-zag pattern. Do not expect to see a snipe like this as they are perfectly camouflaged. They may burst out under your feet.

Following the Grimstone and Sortridge leat round the wide basin below the B3357 road you get good views of one of the Moor's best known features, Vixen Tor. It is a beautiful outcrop of rock, the tallest, from top to bottom, on the Moor. It stands in privately owned land. Time was when you could walk up to and climb it, if you were able, but that, at the time of writing, is all gone. But the story of Vixen Tor lives on.

In a cave at the bottom of the Tor lived a wicked old witch called Vixana (already it seems a bit too convenient). Thin and bent, with scraggly hair that might have been grey if it had been washed, she hated people and enjoyed causing trouble. She also had the power to summon up the mist, so when she saw strangers approaching she could do that and allow them to wander into the bog. From her vantage point up on the Tor (she must have been quite a climber) she would watch their struggles and cackle with delight as they sank to their deaths in the mire.

Came a young man who had in his time done a favour to the pixies and been given as a reward two gifts: ability to see through the mist and a golden ring with which to make himself invisible. Approaching Vixen Tor, he heard the old lady's chuckle of glee, saw through the mist where she sat up on the rock, climbed up behind her and threw her off to her death on the rocks below. (To be read with expression.)

Any comparisons with other personalities present or past are purely in the mind of the reader.

Vixen Tor

14

Having explored the Grimstone and Sortridge leat downstream from Merrivale, I had long neglected the upper reaches, so on a glorious, cloudless January day, totally mis-forecast by a well known broadcasting corporation, I looked at that section. Apart from the cold but sunny day, any boggy patches were frozen solid so walking was no problem. Following the leat upstream you come to the wall of Shillapark farm. The leat goes through but we have to go round the top. It's no problem and as we do, we can see the traces of the higher leat, dug but never used, to replace the lower one. Back down to the flowing leat and immediately after it comes out of the farmland it is crossed by this delightful little clapper under the massive form of Great Mistor. The colourful sheep was there but a few yards upstream. Wonderful what the computer can do.

Following the leat upstream you come to the point where the water is taken off the River Walkham. There is a very small weir in the stream and a cut-water diverting water down the leat. Top left in the picture you can see the river and the point where it was temporarily dammed to send water down the small channel which is still wet, to bypass the construction of the weir.

Bracken
Pteridium aquifolium
A very invasive plant, covering vast areas of the Moor. By excluding light & producing toxins, it inhibits the growth of other plants. While being a food plant for larvae of some moths and butterflies, it is carcinogenic for animals if eaten. The tightly curled young shoots, known as fiddle heads, are considered edible by some people round the world but this may be coincident with increased rates of stomach & oesophageal cancers in far-east countries. Its roots break up old walls and remains of buildings. It can be controlled by repeated trampling & damaging the stems without breaking them off clean.

Having been to the start point of the G&S leat you can walk back along the upper, dry leat but as you approach the Merrivale quarry go back down to the lower one. A slab of granite crosses the leat before you get to the quarry, obviously cut there. The leat then arrives at the top of the quarry, rushes down, partly through a pipe and partly down a steep channel. I cannot recommend following this section. From it you can see the vertical rock-face and the deep, dark lake. The quarry once extracted and cut granite on its own site. For a while it turned to imported stone and now lies abandoned altogether.

After bypassing the quarry, this section of the G&S leat ends by crashing the water down the bank into the more orderly remainder of the leat. It was frozen solid on this occasion. Oh captain Shaw!

A typical clapper bridge on the Grimstone and Sortridge leat, with interested spectator. Along this section of the leat between Merrivale and Windy Post there are several clappers, all within easy reach of the B 3357 road. Below, staff of DNPA repairing the cart-clapper near Windy Post in 1998. Vixen Tor can be seen in the distance.

A number of clappers, like other features of the Moor, need to be repaired from time to time. Thanks to DNPA for this and other pictures.

An unusual view of Vixen Tor, from the Merrivale area, where there are ancient parallel stone rows. Speculate as to their purpose.

Over the G&S leat to Vixen Tor

GRID REFERENCES

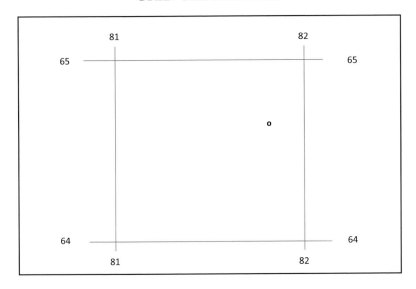

To do Grid References: the map is divided into squares, each 1000x1000 metres. Take the little letter 'O' in the square above. Working from the left at line 81, in your mind's eye divide the square into ten and see how many divisions across find the 'O'. Let us say 8, so from the left we read 818. Then do the same, working upwards from the bottom line, say 646. So our GR is 818646. Always from the left first, then from the bottom, "along the passage and up the stairs". I got O level maths by doing big diagrams.

For the more up-to-date, a yard is 0.9014 metres, an inch (in) is 2.54 cm, a foot (ft) is 0.305 m and a mile is 1.609 km.

Staff of DNPA repairing a little clapper near Babeny. I claim a point for this, having previously noticed the slab lying in the stream, either washed off or vandalised.

THE WALLA BROOK

There are several Walla brooks on the moor. One starts on the western side, in the military ranges and flows down to Lydford gorge. Another starts just on the eastern side of a ridge running up to Hangingstone hill at 624858 amd joins the Teign at Teign e Ver 654871. The similarly named Western Wella brook comes from an area called Snowdon, just north of Huntingdon Warren, at about 665684. I say about because, if you find the source of some streams as shown on the map, moving water can still be seen further up. It depends on recent rainfall.

The Walla Brook of interest here starts below the Warren House Inn at 677809. Flowing south along the flank of the forested area of Soussons Down, it reaches a small clapper giving access (though not public – use the front door) to Runnage farm. A mere 100 yards further downstream is Runnage Bridge.

This is a road bridge built onto an old clapper but reinforced, like several others, according to regulations formulated abroad, to take 42 tonne vehicles. Actually, as the main lintel is a concrete slab and the whole thing is cemented together it no longer qualifies as a clapper, but the old pattern can still be seen.

A few hundred yards on downstream is Pizwell, where there is a small clapper but this is in a wired-off field and not accessible. Another crosses a little stream on the way back to Postbridge.

Grey Wagtail
Motacilla cinerea
Haunts rocky streams, nests in a hole in a river bank, feeds mostly on flies. Despite its name, its most noticeable colour is yellow.

The last clapper on the Wallabrook is below Babeny at 673749. This beautiful little bridge, in its wonderful green setting, is obviously very old and has been very important. It carries the track from Babeny down to the East Dart. The track then goes over stepping stones, up to Brimpt's Farm and on down to Dartmeet. The bridge is in current and frequent use.

Sherrill/Sherwell

Sherrill, also Sherwell, 679748, on the lane to Babeny is a mysterious looking little place, especially on a dull day. I am sure the folk who live there find it idyllic, but it's a long way to the shops. Leave your car well before you get there as there is nowhere to park here or at Babeny unless you have business at either.

There lived in Sherrill a woman of a certain age called Martha Witchalse. She was of a cantankerous nature and whatever her other attributes, she had something like the evil eye. If you crossed her, she had but to wag her finger at you and your days were numbered. Somebody must have liked her though because she had a son. In his teenage years he got to be so badly behaved, with various crimes, that he was banished from the area. Years later, having reformed and grown up, he returned to the area. Meeting an old woman, he did not recognise her. He asked for some water. Throwing a bucket at him she screamed "Go fetch yer own. Tidn my job to fetch water for the likes of you". Perhaps unwisely he said "Had you been nice to me I would have given you this gold coin, but as it is, I shall keep it". She wagged her finger at him. When he told the people he was staying with they feared the worst and well they might because within three days he faded away and died. When they went and told Martha, she realised that she had brought about the death of her own son and she too faded away and died.

The Walla Brook

MEAVY

At the head of Burrator reservoir, 568694, is Norsworthy bridge. There may have been a clapper here but not now. The river Meavy joins the lake here. Follow it upstream and you come to the magnificent clapper bridge. It is unusual in having a parapet. There are also the remains of stepping stones but they were disturbed by forestry workers. There is a good circular walk to be had here. In the main picture you see a track leading away. A signpost points to 'Older Bridge'. Follow the track (it's quite rough) to where it crosses the leat. This is the Devonport leat. Don't give up. This is Older Bridge, though it can't be older than the leat. Then follow the leat downstream - it is flowing strongly – down the cataract, through the woods and back to start.

Older Bridge. This, like the succession of little clappers on the way down the leat, is one of those dull clappers that most might not find interesting, but walk on down and struggle down beside the cataract, enjoy the view over the reservoir and Leather Tor. It's all worth it. And some, as you see, find them quite useful. This is below Cramber Tor. Downhill from the leat is Crazywell Pool, which we will see with Devonport Leat.

Leather Tor Clapper Bridge

Like several others, Leather Tor Clapper has been repaired by DNPA, this time in 1991. Forestry in the area is comparatively new; a photograph early 20thC shows no trees at all.

At 541672 is the small village of Meavy, with the river of the same name flowing past, having filled Burrator reservoir on its way. Take the lane just west of the village, cross the river. Where the lane turns sharp right an even smaller lane runs straight up the slope. Shut the gate. This little lane is sunken, with walls of rock, which show the geology of the area. These stones are metamorphic and shaly. When the great granite plume of what is now Dartmoor was thrust up through the earth's crust, its enormous heat literally cooked the surrounding layers of sandy rock, changing their form and composition.

This deep, rather mysterious little lane leads up to Down Farm and Callisham, and over a small stream a ford and clapper bridge, both marked on the map. It can be more than a bit muddy.

Bird's foot trefoil
lotus corniculatus
'Bacon and egg plant'. Dry seed pods look like birds' feet. Highly poisonous to humans but beneficial for sheep & cattle, relieving parasitic infections & bloating. Plant food for various Blue and Clouded Yellow butterflies. Flowers are nectar source for many adult butterflies and bees.

The clapper bridge and ford near Meavy

Bowerman's Nose
Author

The granite column of Bowerman's Nose, such a famous landmark
and so fragile that we are asked, on a notice nearby, not to climb it.
In the distance Manaton Church, gleaming, even though the sun isn't
shining on it. This is the only sight you are going to see of the author.

BOWERMAN'S NOSE

Bowerman the hunter was a big tall man who spent much time hunting on the Moor with his pack of hounds. He was also a man well liked by the moor folk because of his generosity and kind nature. Well liked, that is, by all except the witches, of whom there were many around the Moor. They hated Bowerman because not only was he not afraid of them, he encouraged others not to fear them either. His lack of fear was perhaps reinforced by the dogs he always kept by him. Out hunting one day, closely pursuing a hare, Bowerman and his hounds ran into a narrow valley where a coven of witches were holding one of their meetings, scattering them and destroying their ceremony. They planned revenge. One of the witches had the power to turn herself into a hare. Her name was, conveniently enough, Levera. Placing herself where Bowerman and his pack could find her, she led them over hill and dale, across streams, round tors, sometimes almost allowing them to catch her, sometimes far ahead. When they were completely exhausted she led them into an ambush of her fellow witches. Shrieking with delight, they cast a powerful spell on him, turning him and his hounds to stone and that is how we find him now, flat cap on and his hounds scattered stonily round his feet. Hearing this, the Moor-folk got together and drove the witches out of Devon and over the water to Wales. That's why Welsh women wear tall pointed hats and why there are no witches in Devon now.

Who's betting on that?

What's wrong with witches? The hatred of them goes back to the arrival of Christianity. A witch was an old lady who had experience of life and a knowledge of herbal medicine. That was in conflict with the new philosophy, which said the best cure for sickness was prayer, and with it payment to the new order of priests. So-called witches represented the old order and, more specifically, they were in competition for the profitable Business. So they had to be disposed of, usually in the most cruel manner, in order to impress the people, keep them subservient and paying tithes to the new Church. That meant torturing and finally burning alive.

What better image of a hare can there be than Albrecht Durer's print of 1503?

THE DART SYSTEM

Upstream from Dartmeet, the East and West Dart rivers act separately, each with its own tributaries and below the meeting place the combined river is too big and prone to flood to permit clapper bridges. Let us start with the West Dart. It rises at about 602817 in a vast, featureless area of the North Moor. Flowing almost due south, it passes one of the most famous features of the Moor, Wistman's Wood. Here, ancient oak trees grow amongst rocks on the west side of a long narrow hill with Longaford and Littaford Tors. The trees are low-growing, contorted and covered with moss. An area has been fenced off to see how plants and trees grow without being grazed by sheep which, being introduced, are not a natural form of control.

The West Dart comes down past Wistman's Wood. Longaford Tor in the distance, with threatening sky ahead. If going walking, never go without water proofs. In Wistman's wood live the Whisht Hounds, with whom the Devil hunts the souls of unbaptized babies over the moor till he drives them over the edge of the Dewer Stone.

The Dipper
cinclus cinclus
Named for its bobbing or curtseying. Hunts under water for larvae, snails and insects, using its wings for propulsion. Makes a domed nest of leaves and grass in a hole in a bank or under a bridge. It is only about 7ins long.

This is the Dewer Stone, at 538639, near Shaugh Prior, at the junction of rivers Plym and Walkham. A notice at the bottom advises those who propose to climb the rock to be sure to have the right equipment. They should also be qualified to do such a climb. It is a very quick trip down to the bottom if you fall off and you are not likely to survive it.

As the West Dart approaches Two Bridges it meets its first tributary, the river Cowsic, which Benjamin Donn in his survey of 1765 calls the West Dart. Upstream on the Cowsic is Beardown clapper, 601754. This very attractive bridge has ten slabs or imposts on five piers and openings and is 37ft long. It is built perilously low over the water and has been washed away by flood , notably in 1873 and 1890. It is now partially protected by great iron rivets joining the slabs. This is one of the original 'Two Bridges'. The problem is; where is the other ? Worth reports that there was a clapper over the West Dart till 1765, replaced by a new bridge in 1772, now itself replaced by the B3357. Certainly Donn shows the track crossing above the confluence. At that presumed point a wall goes right across the field beside the river, ending, despite a gap, at the river bank. That wall is 6ft thick. I propose that it was not just a wall but a causeway across what must have been a very boggy area. Where the wall meets the river there is a great mass of stones, shaped as if to be slabs, lying in the water. If that is not the remains of a second clapper, it can be little else.

If this is just a wall, why is it 6ft thick? Is it more likely a causeway across the marsh?

Did these slab-shaped rocks arrive as they are, across the river, or are they the remains of the old clapper bridge?

Beardown clapper, winter view

Beardown clapper at 601754

At Two Bridges, the bridge built in 1792 to replace the second clapper. This was replaced in turn in 1958 by the present one carrying the B3357.

The view from Two Bridges down the West Dart before it turns eastward towards its meeting with the East Dart.

On its way down to meet the East Dart, the West Dart is joined by the Cherry Brook. This has come through the Powder Mills at 628774. The factory was established by Mr George Frean in 1844 and produced gunpowder. Like any explosives factory, it consisted of a number of small buildings so that, if there was an explosion, the whole lot didn't go up together. The powder was tested from time to time by firing a ball with a given quantity of powder from the testing mortar, which is still there. The work went on until early 20th Century when Dynamite was invented, putting gunpowder out of business. There are two clappers at the site, the bigger and more obvious one supplementing the older, which carried the old Lych way from Bellever to Lydford. Power to drive wheels at the mill was provided by water from a leat which starts on the Dart at about 639814, supplemented by water from the Cherry Brook.

High Brown Fritillary
Argynnis adippe
Brightest of the Fritillaries, this is now quite rare. Mostly found in coppiced woodland, its caterpillar feeds on violets, so environment for these is crucial for the success of the butterfly.

EAST DART

The map shows East Dart Head at about 608856, below the ridge which includes Hangingstone Hill and Cranmere Pool. Benjamin Donn, in his map of 1765, shows the latter like an enormous volcano. In fact you can walk right past it and not notice it. As for the Dart, from the supposed source there is still moving water on the way up the hill almost until it meets the Walla brook going the other way. It depends on recent rainfall. From the same area the rivers Taw, West Okement, Amicombe – later the Tavy and Teign all spring. East Dart wanders down through that huge, mournful and boggy area till it reaches Sandy Hole Pass and becomes more interesting. Shortly after that pass, it goes over the waterfall, its only one, which is more or less impressive according to rainfall. It makes a good walk from Postbridge, either following the river, in which case note the old clappers over the dry leat, or "cut off the corner". In late afternoon the views are spectacular. Sandy Hole Pass also carries the name "the Oak and the Ash". The Oak is growing in a cleft in the rock face on the Eastern side. The Ash is supposed to be on the other side but was not seen.

Fall on the East Dart

Sandy Hole Pass

POSTBRIDGE

First two definitions. On Dartmoor whatever origins of the word, a clapper is a flat stone, so a clapper bridge is one built of just that. The slabs forming the bridge are called 'posts' or 'imposts'. So Postbridge has to do with the bridge, not the mail.

As for the age of this magnificent bridge, arched bridges were being built on the moor by early 15th C so Postbridge must have been in situ before that and could date from at least 1300 CE. The bridge has been repaired at various stages. Some time around 1830 it was reported that one of the two central slabs was lying in the river. A theory is that a farmer had thought it would be a good idea to turn it off, intending it to land on its edge against the piers, thus forming a partial dam and act as a pond for his ducks. Whatever the plan it failed and the stone lay flat on the stream bed until 1879 when quarrymen from Merrivale came and put it back up. One of the stories tells that they put it back upside down. How does anyone know that?

Then in mid 1970s a photograph showed that one of the central piers was leaning and one of the slabs was holding onto the pier by only a couple of inches. So the imposts were raised and the mid-stream piers rebuilt from the river bed and cemented into place with resin. So, as clapper bridges are supposed to be held in place only by their own weight and careful positioning, does Post Bridge still qualify as such? In 1979 DNPA carried out further work and installed the steps leading onto the bridge. I acknowledge here the work by Tom Greeves and Elizabeth Stanbrook for the information.

Everyone goes to Postbridge and it is unusual to find no-one on it. Old photos show flood water right up to the top.

Postbridge

41

THE TROUBLE WITH POSTBRIDGE

As you travel west from Postbridge, past the turning for Bellever, the road slopes steadily uphill for several hundred yards. Do please go very carefully and, especially if you ride a motorcycle, keep a very firm hold on your handlebars. This is the area where the **Hairy Hands** operate. Why they are attracted to motorbikes is hard to tell. They were in the area and working on those driving horses and carts long before the invention of the internal combustion engine. Riders and drivers who survive tell of the appearance of dreadful , disembodied hands, covered in dark hair, which grasp the handlebars, reins or steering wheel and pull the vehicle violently to the side. It crashes into the ditch or the wall and, if not actually killed, the driver can be seriously injured. May I quote from "Devon Ghosts" by Theo Brown, a book published by Jarrolds of Norwich (my mother used to work for Jarrolds): "The prison doctor was asked to go to Postbridge to attend the inquest on a man who had been thrown from his trap and killed – but on another road. Having a motorcycle and side-car, he took two small girls, daughters of a colleague, for the ride. Going down the hill into Postbridge, he was flung off the bike and his neck broken. The children were thrown onto the verge and shaken but not injured. Villagers took charge of them and saw them home."

Walk up the valley, following the East Dart, go over three little clappers on the path after the DNPA information office and the car park. There are more derelict clappers on the leat flanking the far hillside.

As we come down the East Dart between Bellever and Babeny we come to a sad little scene at 662763, called Whiteslade (Snaily House). It's all ruined now, though in sunlight it makes an attractive scene. Some time in the past there lived here two ladies. What relation they had to each other I cannot tell, though some say sisters. They were very private, had no jobs, never went shopping and had no contact with anyone nearby. People were curious, or **Nosy**. So one day, when word got about that the ladies were out, those people broke into the little house to see what went on there. What they found there of significance were stoneware jars containing what the ladies lived on . . .Black slugs.

When the ladies returned and found that their little home had been violated they left and were never seen again.

Wheatear
Oenanthe oenanthe
Summer visitor, its white rump explains its some-time name of white-arse. Nests among rocks, low, flitting flight away when disturbed.

The bridge at Bellever, 658774, deserves consideration on its own. It stands on the East Dart, right beside the road from Postbridge, eventually to Widecombe, and at the eastern edge of Bellever forest. The massive bridge has foundations at each side and two piers in the stream. But where you might expect to find a central slab, there is an obvious gap. If a large slab had been wanted to be used in building somewhere else, it would have made more sense to take one of the end slabs. Nor, if anyone had simply tipped the central slab off, is it to be seen in the stream. In the western pier, however, three slots have been cut. These might have received poles, upon which to lay cross-members and turf to create a temporary but much more easily made crossing. Looking closely at the eastern slab you see that it rests on just one pebble !

Peewit or Lapwing
Vanellus vanellus

Of the Plover family, once very common, now much less so with changes of agricultural practices. Nests on the ground, prefers ploughed land. Aerobatic, swooping flight, a ghostly cry when disturbed at night.

Pink Purslane
Claytonia sibirica
A garden escaper, originally imported from N America. Thrives beside streams. Can be eaten in salads but has little taste. Once used as anti-dandruff wash for hair.

Detail of Bellever bridge, with slots cut in the central pier, possibly to receive poles. The central slab is missing. Below, a main slab or impost rests just on one pebble.

Fly agaric
Amanita muscaria
The typical cartoon toadstool. It is pretty but contains a variety of toxins, causing hallucinations, breathing and circulation disorders and brain damage if eaten. These seen under trees in Lustleigh Cleave.

The Babeny area 672752 provides a pointer to the age of some clappers. Certainly until mid-13th century, the moor came into the parish of Lydford. People who died had to be buried there. That meant that from this area they had to be carried over the East Dart, using the stepping stones at 663757. Carrying a coffin over these would be difficult enough in summer but when the river was high and the stones covered by raging water, impossible. So the procession had to find alternative crossings, most likely downstream at Dartmeet or upstream at Bellever. Either way is longer, so Walter Bronscombe, Bishop of Exeter 1258 to 1280, gave permission for the dead to be buried at Widecombe. As he wrote "Et quod predicta a matrice ecclesia de Lydford **sereno tempore** per **octo**, et **tempestibus** exortis in circuito per **quindecim distant miliaria**." And it doesn't take much latin scholarship to work that out...Actually, it's duodecim miliaria as the corvus fugit.

The clapper bridge at Dartmeet 672732 was washed away in summer 1826 by the same storm that damaged the bridge at Beardown. Trees and other material were washed down against the bridge and built up until the weight of water behind brought it down. It was restored in 1888 and again, partially, by DNPA in 1993.

     Immediately after the East and West Darts meet at Dartmeet, the combined River Dart plunges into the Dart Gorge. This goes down to New Bridge at 711709. The bridge itself seems just a very narrow obstruction when driving over it. But from below it is revealed as a massive structure and makes some fine pictures. There is a good walk up and down the gorge between New Bridge and Dartmeet on the east and north side though the south and west side is rougher and shorter. I have known those who will swim in pools and many enjoy canoeing downstream. But on the Dart, tragedy is never far away. Always remember the old saying "River Dart, River Dart, every year you claim a heart"

In the Dart Gorge

Tom Pearce, Tom Pearce, here's your grey mare

The Red Fox, Vulpes vulpes has overtaken the grey wolf as the most widespread canine in the wild. Distributed throughout the northern hemisphere, red foxes are highly adaptable and occupy territories in deserts and tundra as well as urban areas. They live in family groups in dens and eat most things, including small mammals, fruit, carrion and the contents of dustbins.

Foxes have a wide range of vocal calls including, in season, the vixen's voice that sounds like a human scream. They have long been hunted, with the pretext of vermin control, a myth exposed by reports of hunt staff feeding foxes so as to have them fit and ready to hunt. Urban foxes trapped and carted to countryside cannot cope & die of starvation.

The clapper at Ockery/Oakery
On the road to Princetown

Sheep's bit
Jasione Montana
Typically grows in sandy, acid soils and cliff sides. Though similar, not of the Scabious family

Apparently insignificant, these two clappers carried important tracks. Snap Lane, above, at 533819 is part of the ancient track, the Lych Way, which runs from Bellever, through Powder Mills, across the R Walkham at the head of the Prison Leat, to the Parish town of Lydford.

At 607948, on the northern edge of the Moor, the clapper below carries the Dartmoor Way from Okehampton to Belstone, where it joins the Tarka Trail. The two part company at Sticklepath, Dartmoor Way heading south and Tarka going north to Exmoor.

Sheep's Sorrel
Rumex acetosella
Sour tasting leaves edible as salad or herbal remedy. Nicholas Culpepper (17thC) "of great use against the scurvy".

FERNWORTHY RESERVOIR : some statistics.

A clapper bridge here is one of what one might call 'outliers'. The reservoir was built in 1942 to supply the Torbay area, holds 370 million gallons when full. The dam is 640ft wide by 141ft high. The forest around was planted in 1921 for the Duchy of Cornwall. It measures 576 hectares. The trees are Sitka spruce, Douglas Fir and Japanese Larch. There is a forest trail of 2 ½ miles and the walk round the lake is 3 ½ miles with a disabled path of ¾ mile. 1976 and 2003 were very dry years, when the reservoir ran very low and gave a view of the clapper and the very attractive arched bridge at the bottom. Several small streams feed the reservoir and emerge as the South Teign river, which joins the North Teign at Leigh Bridge, just west of Chagford. I thought I would never see this one but a photo in a regional newspaper sent me (and a lot of others) hurrying up there.

Less than a month later, this was the scene.

Fernworthy reservoir 2003

One of the most famous features of Dartmoor and perhaps the most visited is Haytor. In fact the many visitors can cause erosion and damage to plant life. It is worth going all round these great rocks to see the quarry, long disused, and the railway whose lines are made of granite to take the loads of rock away. A moderate walk takes you to Saddle tor, Holwell Tor and Rippon Tor, from which the views are spectacular. The next few pages offer some sights around Haytor.

Cold Haytor

Gorse
Ulex europaeus
The Fuzz is a very spiny plant which can get to 5 or 6 ft and can make walking very difficult. It also prevents grazing, so is often kept short by burning or 'swaling'. The flowers are seen at any time of year, hence the saying "when the fuzz is in flower, kissing is in season"

Slow worm
Anguis fragilis
A legless lizard, a bright bronze colour. The females often have a dark stripe on the back. Males have larger heads. Well, they would. Hibernates till March. This one was just making its first appearance. They breed in May, young emerge Aug – Sep. They are ovi-viviparous ie born in an egg membrane which breaks open after birth. If captured may shed its tail, which wriggles, distracting the captor while the victim escapes.

Warm Haytor

Hound Tor and Greator Rocks

OUTLIERS

A number of clapper bridges do not share river or leat systems with others and these I call outliers. The one below is near Long Ash, at 549742, over a little tributary of the R Walkham, on a track from Merrivale to Daveytown. Many must walk over without seeing this clapper bridge.

Tormentil
Potentilla erecta
Grows all over the Moor. I have a problem with this plant. Its name, given by W Keble Martin, suggests an upright nature. But it is creeping and looks more like Potentilla reptans, the creeping cinquefoil. No doubt an expert will find fault with this but perhaps more work is needed on both plants. Either way it is a charming feature of the Moor.

Between Princetown and Merrivale, just south of the B3357, is an area I have called, for convenience, Yellowmeade, as there is a farm by that name fairly near. There is a car-park at 561749 with a walled enclosure and trees which can make a dramatic picture. Leading out of the southern wall is a stone gateway and a clapper bridge over the leat that runs right past. On the slopes below that are many archaeological remains, standing stones, circles and two double stone rows in parallel which run west/east, each ending in what looks like a stone pen. They are obviously of great age and one can speculate as to their purpose. I met an American visitor who asked that question. I'm not sure that he was assured by the gruesome suggestion I gave him.

What can the stone rows have been for? In the same area are a standing stone and a stone circle.

Widecombe with twin peaks of Chinkwell & Honeybag Tors

Beside the church, which is dedicated to St Pancras, is a piece of ground originally called Buttes ground. This is where men practised archery after church on Sundays. They had to do that or be fined a halfpenny if they missed the practice. Bows were made from Yew wood, trees being planted in churchyards for that purpose, as well as for any pre-christian beliefs. A famous fair has always been held there. A certain Thomas Cobley had to get there, so borrowed a friend's grey mare to carry him and friends. Uncle Tom didn't live there, he came from Spreyton.

Widecombe, with its magnificent church. Whether you subscribe to religion or not, this church has to be visited. For its tall, elegant tower, it is called the cathedral of the Moor. The barrel vaulting of the ceiling is wonderful, and, in their more rustic way, the bosses are the equal of those in any cathedral. Not least to note are the three hares and the pelican in her piety. And do please make a contribution for the church's upkeep. But our story has to do with the huge panels commemorating the terrible storm of 1638, when the church was struck by lightning in the middle of a service. Extraordinary things happened, and it is worth going to Widecombe to read the report. Among others, one of the pinnacles on the tower was knocked off, fell through the roof and killed several people.

But, according to legend, in the congregation that day was one Jan Reynolds. The tone of voice should get mysterious at this stage. His mind was no doubt on other things. Seven years previous, to the day, he had met a stranger who had promised him seven years good fortune with the cards. And he had those cards with him that day. On that day a stranger set out on a journey to Widecombe. At Poundsgate he called in at the pub, the Tavistock Inn. I have checked that there was a pub here then. There's been one there for 400 years. Having ordered a pint of their best, as the ale went down his throat it **hissed**! (*pause for effect*)and when he put his tankard back on the bar it left a round burn mark. It is still there. I have seen it. And although the bar-top is actually new, the mark seems to have transferred itself from the old one. Continuing his journey, the stranger was seen going through Ponsworthy.

Arriving at Widecombe, the rider tethered his horse to the top of the tower – it must have been quite some horse – went inside, **seized** Mr Reynolds, who must have realised at that stage, and a bit too late, that his seven years were up, and rode off with him across the moor. By now Mr Reynolds must have realised who his captor was and where they were heading. As he was carried across the moor he dropped those cards, and the aces fell on Birch Tor, across the valley from the Warren House Inn. Look across and you can see them, now rather bigger and enclosed by stone walls. The heart and the diamond are clear enough but the club and spade need a bit more imagination to accept them. It is as true today as it ever was, that if something sounds too good to be true, it probably is.

A little aqueduct takes the G&S leat over the stream in Beckamoor Coombe

On the slope of Birch Tor, the Ace of Diamonds

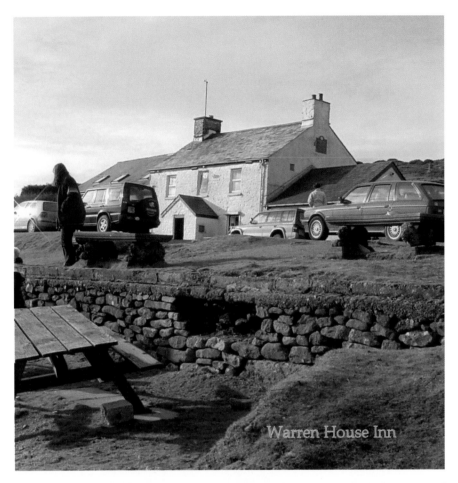

Warren House Inn

While we're gazing across the valley at the stone-walled playing cards of Mr Jan Reynolds, dropped on his way to the nether regions aboard the devil's horse, remember that the Warren House Inn was not always on the side of the road it now occupies. It used at one time to be the other side.

One bitter winter, years ago, a traveller beating his way across the moor could go no further so he booked in at the Inn and was given a room upstairs. In the room was a large wooden chest. Curiosity got the better of him, so he looked inside. A corpse! Rushes downstairs to tell the management, to be told " Oh yes, that's grandfather. The ground's too hard frozen to bury him just yet but as soon as it all thaws we'll dig him in." to be fair to the Warren House, it's a story told about a number of isolated Inns around the Country.

THE BLACKABROOK AND THE PRISON LEAT

The Blackabrook starts north of Princetown, behind the charmingly named Black Dunghill at 580778, flows south through the prison grounds, turns left and joins the West Dart. Its first crossing is the clapper at 577759. One of the writers on the Moor, early 20th C, reports that the bridge is ruined and lying in the stream. Thanks to the efforts of the DNPA it is now enjoying a new life, though it still clings to its eastern pier only by its fingertips. It's one of those odd bridges which don't obviously seem to lead anywhere.

Across the frozen wastes you can see the line of trees marking the B3357. Where the Blackabrook goes under the road there is just room for one car. Look over the new bridge's parapet to see the ruined old clapper which carried the ancient track across the Moor.

Staff of DNPA repairing the clapper on the Blackabrook in 2000

Very close to the clapper is Fitz's/Fice's well. This is in the prison grounds but there is public access. The main wall protects the actual well. Back in the 16th C Sir John Fitz and 'his Lady' (who she?) were riding on the Moor when they became 'Pixie-led' or 'lost'. Coming upon this spring, they drank from it, the mist cleared and they found their way home. Sir John returned to the site, had a little wall built round the spring, with a capping stone over the entrance, inscribed 'JF 1568'. The letters are just visible. The main wall surrounding the well was added later. Ever since, the water has been regarded as beneficial for eye problems and people make pilgrimages there, sometimes leaving little gifts of money. You have to get down on your knees to reach the water, which is beautifully clear, but as the field above is well populated by sheep, and mats of algae float on the surface, I didn't find it necessary to drink it.

Having done a talk at Dunchideock, I had a call from a lady there, asking for an 8-figure grid reference of the well. Did I know that round Dunchideock there are springs with similar properties? I did not, but look in any large dictionary for the word Treacle and you find 'an archaic term for a beneficial salve'. So that explains the Treacle Mines of Dunchideock.

The prison leat takes its water from the junction of the River Walkham and Spriddle Lake 575795. 100 yards or so south is a clapper and this beautiful little arched bridge, probably built by French POWs. It carries the very important ancient track across the Moor from Bellever to Lydford.

You cannot deal with this leat and Dartmoor Prison without reviewing the career of Thomas Tyrwitt (1764 – 1833), pronounced Tirrett, its founder. He was educated at Eton and Oxford, where he was introduced to the Prince of Wales, who immediately appointed him private secretary and member of the Prince's council. Quite why this sudden adoption is not reported but Tyrwitt was described as 'the Prince's very disinterested little friend' and 'his chubby, red, smooth face and stumpy person add to the ridicule of his manner and affected softness of voice and air'. Suffice it to say that he never married. But he must have been no fool, because, having received a grant of 2500 acres on Dartmoor, he first had himself a house – Tor Royal – built, set about farming on the Moor and established the Prison and the community around it. This was first for American prisoners, later for French ones and eventually for home-grown criminals. Another scheme, beset by difficulties, was the construction of a railway from Plymouth to Princetown.

Tom Tyrwitt was elected MP for Okehamptom and later for Plymouth, was made Secretary and Auditor to the Duchy and Lord Warden of the Stannaries, in which post he succeeded Lord Dartmouth, whose descendant now defends the UK's interests in Brussels. He spent much of his parliamentary career working in the interests of the Prince, later Regent and George IV. Towards the end of his career and perhaps as a reward for his services he was appointed Lord Warden of the Black Rod, for which post it was necessary to be a Knight, so he was given that honour. The Royal family, no strangers to rudeness then or now, called him 'June the 23rd' or 'the shortest Knight'

Some sort of scandal arose in 1819 which caused him to 'go to ground' for a while. Nowadays they go to spend time with their families. Whether it was to do with card playing or 'some sexual transgression' is not clear but he survived it, served 20 more years as Black Rod and died in 1833, in Calais, relatively poor.

HUNTINGDON

On the river Avon there is only one clapper but that one is magnificent. It stands at 658662, a few hundred yards upstream from Huntingdon Cross. To get there you have to park at Shipley Bridge 681629 and walk up the road to the Avon Dam. There is nowhere to park there. An alternative might be from Cross Furzes 699668 and take the track westwards through Lud gate 684673.

Between the Avon and the Western Wella brook is Huntingdon Warren, still marked as not being access land. The bridge was installed by Mr John Michelmore, early 19th C. He had the lease of the Warren area, presumably to raise rabbits. He obviously found that rabbits didn't pay. Even now it is known as the eighteen month in and out business. So towards the end of his lease he sold the remainder to friends who happened to own a pack of hounds. That great authority on the Moor, William Crossing, in his book 'the Dartmoor Worker', reports that 'Huntingdon Warren is leased to the Dartmoor Hunt at a nominal rent for the protection of foxes'. Which, if they are now to be 'protected', gives the lie to claims that hunting is done to control pests. They are protected in order to have them available to hunt.

The 2010 picture shows the Avon after days of torrential rain. I still prefer the old picture despite less water and fewer megapics.

Huntingdon Warren clapper, River Avon

Running round the southern curve of Huntingdon Warren are several parallel leats, which took water from the Avon to farm buildings. They are all dry now, but crossed by a number of small clappers. As there are so many they can only have been to allow the bunnies to cross. The subject may be ordinary but the light made the picture wonderful.

The Western Wella brook, on the eastern side of Huntingdon warren, is crossed by a cart clapper carrying the track back to Lud gate and off the Moor.

The clapper at Huntingdon Warren shows the 'feather and tare' method of splitting rocks. Holes were drilled along the desired line, iron leaves were inserted, then spikes driven in, causing a split along the line.

Below, down the R Avon to the reservoir. The remains of ancient settlements to be seen on the far hillside to the left.

KINGSETT DOWN

Friendship mine, Wheal Betsy and Wheal Jewell were copper mines in the long valley beside the A386 as it approaches Mary Tavy. Wheal Friendship was partly powered by steam engine and the smoke and steam emanating from that, with the scarcely controlled tipping of waste, combined to produce a scene of squalor. Power was also provided by water wheels, one at 50ft diameter, described as the largest in the Kingdom. That was only one of 17 working in the site. Although all this was beside the Cholwell brook, that provided nowhere near enough water, so a leat was constructed to bring water from the river Tavy, in Tavy Cleave. The leat still flows, now supplying water to a reservoir on Kingsett Down in square 5281, and provides a useful track up into Tavy Cleave, a walk which is highly recommended.

Tracks across Kingsett Down use the clapper at 527827 over the leat which is lined with stone under the bridge. From that area there is a wonderful view up onto the moor over the Tavy and Baggator Brook, centred on the circular South Common Plantation.

The clapper over Wheal Friendship leat on KingsetttDown.

Speckled Wood butterfly
Pararge aegeria
To be seen in dappled sunlight in woodland clearings and lanes. (and my garden) Feeds, not on flowers, but on aphids' honeydew. So they are good for something! Caterpillar feeds on grasses, especially couch grass.

Up onto the Moor from Kingsett Down

73

Two miserable little clappers, unrelated outliers, attractive only to the truly committed : Cudliptown, left, at 524787, which is dull in winter and obscured by vegetation in summer.

And Wapsworthy, right, at 538802, on the entry to a farm and may not even be accessible though marked 'fb' on the map.

The much more attractive clapper below, unusual in having railings, is at Harbourneford, 718624. The R Harbourne starts up on Lambs Down (see the section on Dean Burn) and joins the Dart at Tuckenhay, near Totnes.

Two more outliers, close but not connected. The one above is at Harford, over the Butter Brook, 641592. There is also a very small clapper over a tiny leat just up hill. They give access to a long walk along the huge ridge from Western Beacon in the south through Three Barrows and on up to Huntingdon Warren, Ryder's Hill and Holne moor. That is a walk for the very fit and well equipped. Going West from Harford is a small but attractive road with a side track to a clapper attached to a wall at 629595.

Several streams run into Burrator reservoir, including the R Meavy and this one, the Narrator brook. Two little bridges cross this, the one above at 578687, regrettably only partly there now but it is marked on the map, as is the one below, further upstream at 586684. This looks like any old rock but it crosses the stream and has been put there to do that. It is a bridge. It also shows that your photographer is not the only madman out on a cold day. This is in an area teeming with little field walls and mine workings that I call the Badlands

New Bridge at 597904

SOME DARTMOOR TERMS

Some words on Dartmoor have meanings different from those elsewhere.

Beare	A wood or copse.
Black	Anglo-saxon Blaec, modern Bleak, pale or colourless.
Bottom	Broad, shallow valley.
Bull's eye	A stone across a narrowed part of a leat with a one-inch hole drilled through to ration water supply.
Clapper	A flat stone.
Cleave	Cliff.
Cist / Kistvaen	A stone burial chamber, probably originally covered with earth.
Clitter	A mass of boulders on a hillside below a Tor which has been broken down over millions of years, mostly by frost.
Cornditch	A wall, with a ditch dug on its outside, the spoil being dumped on the inside and level with the top. That's a Ha Ha.
Cut	A track cut down through peat to hard substrate.
Fuzz	Gorse.
Fern (Vern)	Bracken.
Gert	A deep scar in a hillside, the result of open-cast mining.
Growan	A gravel-like stuff beneath turf surface, decomposed granite.
Lake	A tributary stream.
Man	Maen a standing stone.
Launder	A wooden trough fitted with sluice gate for rationing water.
Newtake	An area of land, up to 8 acres, enclosed from the rough moorland by a tenant farmer, held by right established by two previous generations' occupation of the land.
Pool	A lake.
Pound	A stone-walled enclosure for keeping stray cattle. But also surrounding settlements with huts, eg Grimspound, probably for defensive purposes.
Reave	Ancient boundary, a bank of earth and stone.
Row	Rough.
Traw	Trough. A steep sided valley.
Wheal	A mine, never "a" wheal, often given female names Sometimes spelt Huel in Cornish, ie a Hole, which is basically what a mine is.
Walla	Celtic, possibly Willow or Tumbling Brook.

THE DEAN BURN

The Dean Burn rises at a spring 681672, at the edge of private land. It then goes down, mostly through woodland till it flows into the Dart at Buckfastleigh. A surprising amount of detail in this work surrounds such a small stream. Start by taking a small lane going west out of Buckfastleigh, following a sign to Wallaford. Given the number of Walla Brooks on the moor one might expect another one to be involved here but the map shows none. Local knowledge may have other information. The lane goes up, seemingly for ever, to a crossroads at 700667. Here are three metalled lanes and a fourth, a very rocky track, goes down to the Dean Burn. Here is a clapper bridge which spans the stream and is very low over the water. Floods have obviously washed it away a number of times and each time its repair date is carved in the stone. You get a clear view of the site in the winter, but in summer, when the leaves are out it is a very dimpsy little place, like a number of such bridges. Those who know ancient Greek poetry will remember that some of it, besides rhyme and metre, had to follow a rhythm which went "Down in a deep dark dell, sat an old cow chewing a beanstalk". Well, here is the deep dark dell; the old cow comes later.

Grey Heron
Ardea cinerea
Stalks shallow water, hunting fish, frogs, any small prey. Nests in trees in colonies, voice seldom used but an awful screech.

Cross Furze, Dean Burn

Large Blue butterfly
Phengaris amnion
Most extraordinary life pattern. Caterpillar feeds on thyme for about 3 weeks. Drops off, found by red ant. Secretes honeydew, which ants love. Ant carries caterpillar into nest, where it gives more honeydew for ants, but eats the ants' eggs.

They probably think the sacrifice worthwhile. Caterpillar pupates in ants' nest, emerges as butterfly. Ants then escort to suitable bush & protect it while drying out.

Cross over the Dean Burn and take the track which bears left and leads up to Lambs Down. It is rather muddy. A few hundred yards up the hill you come to a clump of beeches with the remains of old walls. This is marked on the map as "Farmstead" in gothic type. Here, even when it was already in a state of decay, there lived an old miser called Jan Meddler. One day a beggar came by and, seeing Jan messing about in what passed for a garden, asked for some money. In a rare moment of generosity, Jan gave him a coin. Looking at the coin and seeing it apparently as a farthing (you remember those) he threw it on the rubbish heap and went on his way. Quite which was the rubbish heap you may wonder. Anyway, Jan goes indoors to check over his hoard of gold coins : finds one missing ! "Expletive deleted! I've given that beggar a gold coin". He spent the rest of his life scrabbling about in the rubbish heap looking for it and now, on moonlit nights, the ghostly form of Jan Meddler may be seen scrabbling about in the ghostly rubbish heap, looking for the ghostly gold coin.

The Raven
Corvus corax
Feeds on dead sheep and other animals but also live rabbits, hedgehogs and rats, almost anything. In spring gives aerobatic displays. Nests on rock ledges or trees. Distinctive voice says 'Cronk'.

The clump of beeches marks the ruined farm of Jan Meddler

Further down the Dean Burn valley is the little hamlet of Dean Combe. Here in, days gone by, lived a man called Thomas Knowles. He was a weaver, and as such well regarded. But also a bad tempered person, not popular in the area. He had two sons who were intended to take over the business, but he would never hand over, and one son died before he did. When he did eventually die he was buried at Dean Prior church. You pass this beside the A38 on the way to Plymouth, after Buckfastleigh. His surviving son Philip threw a party and prepared to carry on the trade.

Next morning Philip heard a noise from the upstairs weaving room. Creeping up the stairs, he looked through a crack in the door. There, at the loom, was his father. Having been buried the day before. This is work for the vicar he says and hurries off to the church. The vicar knows about this sort of thing, so takes a handful of earth from the churchyard. Back at the cottage, the vicar calls from the bottom of the stairs, in a vicar-like voice you may use as you like, " Mr Knowles ; come down here!" In a crotchety voice came the reply "I can't come. I haven't finished !" "Yes you have. Come down this minute" and down the stairs comes the ghostly form of Thomas Knowles. The vicar throws the handful of earth in his face, whereupon he turns into a great black dog. (There are black dogs all over Dartmoor.)

The three, Vicar, Philip Knowles and the dog, go down to the Dean Burn. There, there is a waterfall pouring into a pool. The vicar finds a little nutshell with a hole in it. Giving this to the dog, he says "Use this to empty the pool. When you have finished you may rest."

Plentifully fed from the moor above, the stream still flows on. Sadly, I found no name of Knowles on any gravestone at Dean Prior Church.

HEATHER comes in two main varieties. This is *Calluna vulgaris*, or LING. It is a food source for sheep, deer and grouse and larvae of various moths and butterflies. Also a source of highly valued honey, thixotropic, hence difficult to extract, so often sold as comb honey. Hives are moved to moorland areas for summer months.

Painted Lady
Vanessa cardui
Summer visitor from N Africa. Many seen in transit through Gibraltar. Caterpillar feeds on thistles. This one photographed on Buddleia, Wheal Betsy, Mary Tavy.

This is the Weaver's cottage, at Dean Combe. It may be a replacement for the original. If you follow up these stories, bear in mind that Dean Combe is a very small place. There is nowhere to park and lanes leading out of the hamlet go on for miles before you find somewhere to turn round. Better to park long before you get there and enjoy the walk beside the Dean Burn on the way. Beside the A38, past Buckfastleigh, on the way to Plymouth, stands Dean Prior church. I found no sign of the name 'Knowles' on any gravestone. A previous incumbent of Dean Prior church was Robert Herrick 1591 – 1674, who was a poet as well as a priest. He lost his position during Cromwell's Commonwealth, owing to his Royalist persuasion. On Restoration, Charles II gave him the post back. Among his works are 'Cherry ripe . . .', 'Gather ye rose buds while ye may . . .' and 'a sweet disorder in the dress . . .' (look it up). The general message of his work seems to be that life is short, the world is beautiful, love is splendid and we must make use of the short time we have to make the most of it. Which makes him more or less a Humanist. He remained a bachelor all his life.

Wren
Troglodytes troglodytes
Almost the smallest resident bird, has, size for size, the loudest song and the longest name. Male makes several domed nests, female selects the one she prefers. In winter numbers cluster together in nest for warmth and shelter.

Down the Dean Burn is Buckfastleigh, where the church stands on top of the hill, well outside the village, away from view. Being so private, it was used for some years for satanic practices, culminating in being burnt down in 1992. The spire & bells were restored in 1996.

Outside the main entrance to the church stands this little building. Unlike the church it is in perfect repair, not a slate missing, not a flaw in the paintwork, not a dead leaf to be seen. A door at the back is locked and on the side facing the church an iron grille forms part of the wall. This is the tomb of Squire Richard Cabell.

Mr Cabell/Capel lived at Brook Manor, which is up the valley towards Holne. He was greatly feared and was reputed to capture village maidens and keep them locked up for his pleasure in Hawson Court, across the valley, which he also owned, away from the eyes of Mrs Cabell. When he died in 1677, he was buried, some say 12ft deep, with a great stone on his head and the tomb over that, capped with yet another granite slab and iron railings in front. Because ghosts cannot pass iron (they do say). During the 39-45 war, when railings had to go for armaments, no-one allowed these ones to go. Now, on dark nights, flickering lights may be seen and Squire Cabell goes out hunting with his pack of black hounds. Can't pass iron? This story and others told him on a visit to the area may have inspired Conan Doyle to create the Hound of the Baskervilles, as the coachman who met him at the station was Mr Baskerville. I am told that there is at least one by that name in the churchyard.

Above the Dean Burn a rainbow shone against the dark sky. Up on Lambs Down a herd of these amiable creatures seemed as surprised to see me as I was them. This is where the Harbourne River starts, at 696651, makes its way down through Harbourneford, not to be confused with Harbertonford, and on to join the Dart at Tuckenhay, near Totnes.

A Marsh orchid
Dactylorhiza ericetorum

Black Tor 567895 overlooks Black Tor Beare or Copse, one of the ancient oak woods of Dartmoor.

West Okement river
below Black Tor Beare

Below, on a misty autumn day, the gorse is in flower. The East Dart follows the far valley, and a ruined clapper spans the leat which skirted the hillside , left of the valley, taking water to the Powder Mills. All its clappers are now ruined.

Sourton

This story begins at Sourton (pronounced Sorton) between Okehampton and Tavistock. The inn has been there since at least 1290. It is also the start of some good walks and cycle rides. Visit the church. The ceiling is impressive. Walk up the lane past the church, through the moor gate and up past Sourton Tors – it's more a jumble of rocks. Keep going up. We are going up to Corn Ridge, an extension northwards of Amicombe Hill to meet, back in the 13th C, Walter Bronscombe, bishop of Exeter from 1257 to 1280. His remains lie in this magnificent tomb in the Lady chapel, Exeter cathedral.

Walking on up past Sourton Tors, reflect a moment on Bishop Bronscombe. Having seen the works at Salisbury, he oversaw the third major rebuild of Exeter cathedral, including the construction of the Lady chapel where he now lies. His effigy, carved in black basalt and painted, is between the Lady chapel and St Gabriel's chapel. The colours are those put on when it was made. He it was who gave permission for the dead to be buried at Widecombe when the Dart was in such high flood that they could not be carried over on their way to Lydford, as before. We will meet him again shortly. After Sourton Tors we go over a fairly flat section, with magnificent views north and west off the Moor.

We have to cross some track marks. This is the ancient route between Okehampton and Tavistock, called the King's Way. Here, on dark nights, rides Lady Mary Howard, who lived at Walredden Manor, near Tavistock. In her time she disposed of three husbands and several children. Now she rides in a coach made of the bones of her murdered husbands, driven by a headless coachman and accompanied by the inevitable great black dog (one of the many around Dartmoor), to Okehampton Castle. It is a very grassy place and well worth visiting. There, the black dog (why him ?) has to pluck one blade of grass per visit and when he has cleared the lot the entourage may all rest.

Okehampton Castle

Begun after 1066 as a motte and bailey castle, it was never used as a defensive site. It was first occupied by the Courtney family who converted it into a splendid residence and status symbol until Henry de Courteney fell foul of Henry VIII and was 'attainted', losing his castle, lands and head. After that the castle fell into disuse and ruin. It is now said to be haunted and we know who by!

The King's Way
Meldon Reservoir

Amicombe Hill
Meldon reservoir

DARTMOOR NATIONAL PARK is a special purpose local authority created under the Environment Act 1995 as a free-standing local authority, employing around 150 staff and is governed by 22 appointed members. Before 1995 it was administered as part of Devon County Council. The Authority's duties, responsibilities and powers are set out in the 1995 Act and include two principal duties, namely : to conserve and enhance the natural beauty, wildlife and cultural heritage of the National Park and to promote opportunities for the understanding and enjoyment of the special qualities of the Park by the public. In pursuing the statutory powers of the national Park, the Authority has the 'socio-economic' duty to foster the well-being of communities within the National Park.

Bishop Walter Bronscombe and his chaplain had been riding across the Moor for whatever purpose, perhaps a diocesan visit. They were very tired and hungry. They were also, and I hesitate to say it in view of their doubtless sincere beliefs, pixie-led or in other words, Lost. In fact, as we have already established the age of it, they just had to go straight down the hill and call at the inn. It seems they didn't know that. "Oh my Lord, says the chaplain, I'm so hungry, I'd do anything for some bread and cheese right now!" "Anything!"says the bishop "remember that our Lord was tempted with the gift of food when in the desert". At that moment a stranger appeared. They do on Dartmoor; you may think you are the only one for miles but someone will appear on the skyline. This one was carrying a large haversack and walking in a **strange manner**. He approaches our two. "My good sir" says the bishop, who was getting on a bit by now and sounds rather like an aged relation of mine, "you wouldn't by any chance have any food with you? Hm?" "Oh yes" says the stranger "I have bread and cheese. " Oh, we would be happy to pay" "No need to pay" says the stranger, in a voice you may have heard in a film about Richard III, "all you need to do is to climb off your horse, doff your cap and address me as **Master**". "Well, it seems a small price to pay" says the bishop, and was half way off his horse when the chaplain grabs his sleeve and whispered loudly "My Lord, LOOK AT HIS FEET!". At the sight of his cloven hoofs the bishop made a great sign of the cross at him and the stranger instantly disappeared, leaving behind him the bread and cheese, turned to granite, and there they stand to this day, at 553891, called...
...**Branscombe's loaf**

Foxglove
digitalis purpurea
Most often found on broken ground & cleared woodland. Very toxic; one nibble can cause death by heart failure, though medicines extracted for heart disease & epilepsy. Food plant for larvae of some moths.

The little bridge above was found in the course of a walk looking for other things. It is to be found at 752788, where a track crosses the Beckabrook and goes up past Hound Tor and the medieval village, which we had better see. The clapper below is over a tributary of the same stream, above Becky Falls, at 758802, on one of the walks round the park. Follow the yellow arrow.

Medieval village, Hound Tor

TROWLESWORTHY WARREN

The leat running across the western slope of Trowlesworthy Warren takes its water from the river Plym near Ditsworthy Farmhouse at 587663. The house, long since abandoned as a farm but used for adventure training now, presents about as miserable and bleak a scene as one could wish to find. Near the house a cart clapper crosses the leat which then goes round the Warren and on to deliver water to the clay works at Lee Moor. It was built in the 1830s for that purpose, being cut by Mr Wm Phillips. Along the leat are no less than twenty-one clappers of various sizes giving access for livestock to grazing areas. As to the nature of that livestock, it has to be assumed, given the name of the place, that they were rabbits.

A typical clapper over the leat. I'll spare you the rest of them as they are all much the same. Pink granite was quarried at Trowlesworthy Tor for use in London.

At the southern end of the leat look over the edge and see this moon-like vista. This is where the fine white clay for the potteries of Stoke on Trent came from. Other uses of china clay are legion, from insulators to cosmetics, pills and paper.

Cart clapper, Trowlesworthy Warren leat

The cart clapper near Ditsworthy Warren House takes the track over the leat and down to a ford over the river Plym.

With some older digital cameras there was a delay between pressing the button and getting a picture. You had to shoot before the subject got to the desired position. A certain amount of guesswork was involved. Sorry about the light but this one could not be left out.

Foxworthy upstream

FOXWORTHY BRIDGE

This magnificent clapper bridge is at 758821, over the River Bovey. There are several ways to get there, but a very satisfactory one is to start from Lustleigh, after lunch in the pub or to end up there after your walk. A track leads up along the eastern side of the Cleave to the bridge. Being made of such massive rocks it may come as a surprise to hear that the biggest of them, the western impost, has in its time been washed off by floodwater and is now supported by a concrete lintel. Continue past the bridge, up the lane to Peck Farm, then back to start along the top. On the way you pass Hunter's Tor. There you may see the earthworks of an ancient fort, said to be Roman. That's not all you may see because some have seen, at suitable times, a platoon of Roman soldiers marching out.

Hunter's Tor

Foxworthy Downstream

MORE OUTLIERS

There are three small clappers in the same area; Hurston, Jurston and Langaford bridge, all crossing the same small stream. Approach all via the B3212 at Lettaford Cross 710841, then map read round the lanes. Langaford bridge, as shown on the map, carries the actual road over a stream which eventually joins the West Webburn. There is a space to park nearby. Look over the west side parapet and see, amongst the undergrowth, better seen when the leaves have fallen, and long bypassed, this delightful little clapper bridge. It is at 702849.

Langaford bridge

And, to give access to this pretty scene, a gate has been installed beside the road bridge, with an extra clapper below. Some authorities are so considerate !

Two little outlying bridges, quite closely related, cross the stream that goes down to Langaford bridge and on to the East Webburn. Hurston, above, at 688844 and Jurston, below, at 697844

Lower Cator

LOWER CATOR

A pair of clappers cross the West Webburn River at Lower Cator, 689764. One carries a "new" road, the other, in our main picture, has been bypassed and left to rest, unused, in an idyllic scene, like another French impressionist painting. It is 9ft long, and only nine inches thick, a delicate rustic marvel. Sitting on it, you can survey the other, which, though modernised, is also a pleasant sight. How old either of them is, is anyone's guess.

The road bridge at Lower Cator, below; safety demands railings, in which it resembles the clapper at Harbourneford.

The Oak and the Ash. In considering Dartmoor's ancient oak woods, this is surely the smallest, being only one tree and that surviving only by growing in a rock pocket, out of reach of sheep. This is where the East Dart comes through Sandy Hole Pass, 622813. The Ash is supposed to be on the other side of the river, but there is no sign of it.

Steeperton Tor

This beautiful, conical Tor is at 619888. The young river Taw, starting near Cranmere Pool, comes down the little gorge to the right of the Tor. At the head of the gorge are the remains of an old clapper, now lining a ford on a military track.

One of those Tall Tales. Take the lane running north from Ivybridge to the moor gate at 625616. Go up the hill north-eastwards to the top. There is a pile of stones. In the middle is square space. It clearly has been some sort of a shelter. From the top the views over the moor are stunning. It is called Hillson's House 636623

Years ago, a baby was found abandoned on the hill top. Taken in and raised by local people, he acquired the name of Hill Son. Grown up, he returned to the spot, built himself a little house and took up the trade of clock-making. No power, no water, no communications and all in a building about 8 by 8ft square. But it is said that some of his 8-day clocks can still be seen in the area. Believe that...

On the way back, walk down Stall Down and admire one of the longest stone rows on the Moor.

Stone Row, Stall Down

The Whooping rock, on Easdon Tor, 729823 off the lane from Widecombe to Chagford. This lane is the original "all along downalong outalong lea". The views from Easdon Tor are stunning. Not, perhaps, to children suffering from whooping cough, who were taken up there and made to run around the rock three times. Maybe if the whooping cough didn't get them the run might have. Look back across the valley to see Haytor, Hound Tor, between them Greator rocks and, in a jumble of rocks, Bowerman's Nose, which we saw in page 29

Stonechat
Saxicola torquata
Belongs to the thrush family, lives on insects and grubs, including pests which attack sheep. Nest of grass, moss, hair and wool, in gorse bushes. Male keeps guard nearby and scolds intruders with sharp alarm note like pebbles clicking. The Whinchat is similar, though not so colourful and is only a summer visitor.

PLYMOUTH AND DEVONPORT LEATS

By the late 16th Century Plymouth was becoming an important mercantile city. Every gathering of people needs water, and the springs and wells in use till then were fast becoming insufficient. So an act of Parliament of 1585 authorised Plymouth City Corporation to "digge a trenche" to bring water from the river Mewy (now Meavy). The job was given to no less a person than Sir Francis Drake, who was given a grant of £300 to get it done. He didn't do the work of course, though stories went about that he had ridden about on the moor till he found a suitable spring, then turned his horse loose and as he or she galloped home, the water followed. The Devil must have been involved. In fact, as a proven captain, he was well able to manage men and work, so employed Mr Lampan to do the surveying and local tinners to do the digging. Drake cut the first ceremonial turf in December 1590 and the work was finished by April 1591. Ever since, though properly called the Plymouth leat, it has always been known as Drake's leat.

The leat began with a head weir on the Meavy, now beneath the Burrator reservoir. It carried the city's main water supply for 300 years. To increase the leat's efficiency, starting in 1871, the leat was lined with granite slabs – for much of its course within the National Park it still is, though in some places these have been stolen and when it goes off the moor, it disappears altogether, to reappear as traces in Plymouth. By 1900 the whole thing was made redundant by the development of Burrator reservoir and the piped supply of water to the city. Now, as it passes Yelverton and goes round Roborough Down, the leat is still mostly in pristine condition, crossed by several clapper bridges. Whether these were installed at the original time is not clear, as on one bridge the numbers 1893, occupied by moss, can be seen.

Part of Drake's leat as it goes across Roborough Down on the way down to Plymouth. Note the finely cut granite slabs lining the leat.

DEVONPORT LEAT

As Plymouth grew in importance, its docks area grew likewise, with ship building and port facilities and, like Plymouth, needed more water. Plymouth, however, needed all its supply and would not let the dock area have more from the leat, which already had some 27 outlets to local industries. And their refusal was emphatic. In 1762 the famous Dr Johnson was in town and though it is not clear what it had to do with him, except that he had a lot to say about everything, he is reported as saying "these aliens (nowadays the expression is furriners) and upstarts must not be allowed to share Plymouth's water supply. Let them die of thirst ! They shall not have a drop !" He was from Lichfield.

So, in 1793 the Company of Proprietors of Plymouth Dock got powers to build weirs on several Dartmoor streams and bring water to Devonport. Like Drake's leat, parts of this leat can still be seen in Plymouth/Devonport. The leat is still working and is maintained. Starting on the West Dart, across the valley and upstream a bit from Wistmans Wood, it flows as far as the dam of Burrator reservoir, where the water goes into a pipe via Dousland. Thereafter Drake and Devonport leats, both dry, run roughly parallel till, having crossed Roborough Down, they go into private land and disappear. There was a time when, as the leat approached Two Bridges, it was directed up the eastern side of the river Cowsic, where it augmented the flow of water from the head weir there. Later it was found more efficient to build an aqueduct across the lower reach of the Cowsic. This now takes the water, which emerges into the leat which comes down the west side of that stream, through a syphon.

Devonport leat, head weir

Buzzard
buteo buteo
A medium sized raptor, wingspan 1 – 1½ yards. Preys on rabbit, pheasant and other small birds, snakes, lizards & insects. Fiercely territorial, mates for life. Aerobatic displays in spring to attract new mate or reinforce bond with present one. Flight mostly gliding & soaring. "Mewing" cry as it circles in thermals.

Along the stretch of the Devonport leat between its start and Beardown there are a number of clappers, both single and for carts. Most also give views across the valley of the West Dart to Wistman's Wood and Longaford Tor above it. The wood is in three main parts, South, Middle and North woods. The gnarled and stunted trees give an air of great antiquity and mystery. And well they might, for in these woods are kept the Whisht hounds with whom the devil hunts the souls of unbaptized babies across the moor till they fall to their deaths (their second one, since they are already dead) over the huge granite cliff of the Dewerstone, to be found at the meeting of the Plym and Walkham rivers. There is a very good walk from the park below the Dewerstone, up the hill through the woods, seeing the many archaeological remains on the way. From the top follow the direction of the Plym to Cadover bridge, cross and come back on the other side. Above the Dewerstone is an insignificant rock outcrop, hardly deserving the title of Tor, inscribed with names. As usual with Victorians, despite the undesirability of graffiti, the lettering is beautifully done. One of the names is N T Carrington. His father apprenticed him to the Plymouth Dockyard but he quit because he couldn't stand the foul language of the dockers. So he joined the Navy ! He was present at the battle of Trafalgar. When his captain heard he wrote poetry he was told to go and find another more suitable job. He took up teaching, spent what spare time he had on the moor and writing poetry best measured by the yard, or even the mile, for its quality.

From Wistman's Wood, Devonport leat across the valley.

Across the valley from Wistmans Wood, the sheep find a clapper useful for crossing the leat as it goes down towards Beardown.

The main picture (p 112) shows one of the smaller offshoots of Wistman's wood, with a view across the West Dart valley. The straight, horizontal line running across the far hillside is the Devonport leat. The leat and the West Dart now go down to Two Bridges. Your photographer went out in all weathers.

After Two Bridges Devonport leat and the West Dart part company. Dart goes down to Dartmeet, where we see the ancient clapper pictured elsewhere. The leat goes on a loop through private farmland, round Princetown and the Prison. There are clappers on the way but I would not want anyone to trespass in searching for them. So from Tor Royal, the house built for Mr Tyrwhitt, the leat flows almost south, first to Peat Cot. This curious little place was established soon after the leat was completed, and it was occupied by members of the Worth family for over two hundred years. Among them was Richard Hansworth Worth (1868 – 1950), one of Dartmoor's noted historians, with books to his credit. As it goes round the sharp little re-entrant that encloses Peat Cot, the leat is crossed by several small clappers and a cart clapper gives access from the farm up to the Princetown road. The main house is remarkable, being now a sort of pink colour and having Gothic style windows. This, and the presence of a tiny chapel for just one family, probably in view of the hold held over the family by the church.

The farm house at Peat Cot, with its chapel – like windows. Once white, its colour is now debatable. The leat now proceeds along the featureless slope of a hill overlooking the Strane river and comes to Whiteworks and the view over the mysterious, brooding Foxtor Mires.

I make no apology for including these two pictures of roughly the same area. Seen in late summer, the clouds and the play of light on the Moor were quite entrancing. The 'two-slab' clapper in the tight bend of the leat above Whiteworks makes a satisfying picture. Foxtor Mires is a natural basin, surrounded by hills, with only one outlet where the Swincombe plunges down a rocky ravine before reaching its small flood plain. Geographers will recognise that, even in that small area the river starts meandering. So minerals washed out of those hills collected in the basin. Granite, of which the Moor is mostly made, is composed of feldspar, quartz and mica. The feldspar is the most easily broken down by frost and water and collects to form a fine white clay called kaolin. British potters wondered for generations how the Chinese made such beautiful white wares. They used a clay called petuntse. Much searching eventually found deposits of something very close to that in Cornwall and parts of Devon. They were exploited soon enough by Josiah Spode and a whole industry of clay extraction and pottery manufacture began. Back to Foxtor Mires : on the deposits of clay, moss grew, ever thicker and floating on water. As the top layers grew, the bottom ones decayed and turned to peat. In bogs such as Foxtor Mires this floating surface can be very dangerous and many's the tale of walkers and even riders falling through thinner patches, drowning in the soft mud and water, covered by the peat and never seen sight nor sign of again.

These famous Mires are without doubt the inspiration for the Grimpen Mire in Conan Doyle's Hound of the Baskervilles. Whiteworks, now more black than white, was the site of china clay extraction and also of tin mining. The owners of the mine were responsible for the construction of the road, or rather track, from Norsworthy at the head of Burrator reservoir up to the Princetown road and down to the mine. It was to take the carts of the mine works. It is now very rocky and wouldn't do those carts much good now. There was a scheme to build a dam across where the Swincombe leaves the Mire and form a reservoir which would have held eleven billion gallons of water but that scheme never materialised. Yet.

Common Adder
Viper Vipera berus
A venomous snake, widespread in Europe and all the way to Far East. Not aggressive, only bites in self defense. Bite can be painful but rarely fatal. Feeds on small mammals, lizards, insects. Females breed once in two to three years. Young, ovoviviparous, like slow worms, born in late summer. Found in all terrains but, being cold blooded, must bask in sunshine to get systems working. Hibernates through winter.

115

Cart clapper, Devonport leat, Foxtor Mires

116

Whiteworks and Foxtor Mires and two-slab clapper, across a bend in the Devonport Leat

117

Across Foxtor Mires, on the lower slope of Foxtor at 626703, stands Childe's Tomb. Everyone was a child at some time, but a Childe with an 'e' is an ancient title for the eldest son of a local ruler. Compare Childe Harold, and Childe Lambton, who brought the Lambton Worm home from Europe to terrorise the Durham area. This one was called Ordulf, perhaps alive in 1066, son of an Earl of Devon. Out hunting one bleak winter, he got separated from friends and lost in the snow. Realising that he would be dead by morning, he killed his horse, disembowelled it and sheltered in the stomach cavity. He died anyway. But before doing so he wrote his will in blood on a stone, leaving his lands at Plymstock to whoever should find the body and give it decent burial. The monks of Tavistock set out to find him. The monks of Plymstock, long having had their eyes on those lands, set up an ambush. The Tavistock monks heard about this (HOW ?) , quickly threw a bridge over the R Tavy – one of the fastest flowing streams in England – and got safely home with the body. Question is : having taken the body away, why build a tomb out on the moor? It is quite a deep tomb, lined with great granite slabs. A monument by all means, or a cross perhaps but the place for a tomb is where the body is buried. That's why I use the term Tall Tales. Walking to Childe's tomb, stick to the high ground.

Crazywell Pool is at 582705, between Devonport leat, as it skirts Cramber Tor, and the track up to Older Bridge. As you follow the circular walk from Leather Tor clapper it is worth making a diversion. The pool is never exactly a pretty sight. Some thought it bottomless and tried plumbing its depths with the combined bell-ropes of Walkhampton church but found no bottom. Actually it's about 15ft deep. It is said to be prophetic. On midsummer eve a voice may be heard announcing the name of the next person to die in Walkhampton parish. If you see your reflection in the water on that day it may well be you. The story goes of two young men, who, having drink taken, rode up to the pool on a motorbike, had a swim, crashed on the way home and were both killed. In the course of military training one soldier was drowned crossing it. The moor is the property of the crown. When there is a Duke of Cornwall it, and its profits, go to him. But when there is none, the King may give the stewardship to whomever he likes. Edward II liked his friend Piers Gaveston very much and gave it to him. Edward came to a very sticky end at the hands of the Nobles and Gaveston took refuge on the moor. Being up by Crazywell Pool one day, he met one of those old ladies who have certain powers of foresight. She told him he would be very famous and his head would be held up high. Which it was, not long after, on the walls of Warwick Castle.

The Devonport leat is tipped down the cascade at 575714, into an aqueduct over the R Meavy, and on down the more conventional course. A metal pipe also brings water from a few yards upstream and pours it into the leat. Note the cut slabs of stone lining the leat. The dumps of stone beside the leat further up were for this but never used.

The Gate-keeper
Maniola tithonus
Caterpillar feeds on grasses. The adult is seen in July and August, in grassy rides and hedgerows, feeding on bramble flowers, wood sage and marjoram. Common throughout England and Wales, southern areas of Scotland.

Devonport leat leaves the woods, Far Sheep's Tor

Please think back to the section on Cross Furzes and the ancient Greek verse, and the old cow chewing a beanstalk. Here, at last, as the Devonport leat fizzles out below Yelverton, is that cow. Not with a beanstalk it's true but it was a great moment ! Below is almost the last we see of the Devonport leat as it snakes across the Yelverton golf course on Roborough Down and disappears out of the Moor.

Cart clapper, Drake's leat, Roborough Down. View over to Lee Moor

ROOK TOR

Rook Tor itself is hardly significant, being only on the lower end of a wide spur going up to Penn Beacon at 597628. This clapper, of large stone slabs is only over a ditch, quite close to East Rook Gate, 606616. From all over that hill feature there are wonderful views, eastward over Stall Down, where we find Hillson's House and down to the sea. The simple clapper over a dry leat, much further up the slope may be small but the panorama down to the sea is worth the journey.

Small Tortoiseshell
Aglais urticae
Once very common, now, like all butterflies, much less so. Breeds twice per year, caterpillars feed on nettles, hence the name urticae. This one seen on Ling, mine spoil tips near Mary Tavy

Sundew
Drosera rotundifolia
Lives in marshy areas lacking in nutriments. So it gets its sustenance from "eating" insects. The modified hairs on the leaves are tipped with sweet tasting but sticky globules. A fly lands on this, can't get off. The leaf then slowly rolls up, the fly is trapped and digested.

RUDDYCLEAVE WATER

This little stream is not very long. Its source is in the ominous sounding Blackslade Mire at about 737755. Running south, it goes under a small lane at 735746 on Pudsham Down, where there is a clapper bridge which, like several others, has been reinforced to take those heavy continental lorries which have been directed here by the wonders of modern technology. Beside the copse there is ample parking and the whole is a most delightful site. Also, as with other streams, we are asked not to interfere with fish spawning arrangements by building dams. Further downstream, Ruddycleave Water passes the little settlement of Bowden, at 728737, where it goes under a clapper and creates a scene out of French impressionism. It is best reached by parking at 740743. Follow a wall roughly south and branch off to take the rough track beside Birch Wood. From the hilltop there is a wonderful view down to the coast at Teignmouth. The stream then goes on to join the Dart below Buckland in the Moor.

The clapper on Ruddycleave Water, Bowden

THE VITIFER MINE

This tin mine was in the area of square 6881 on the slope of Birch Tor, across the valley from the Warren House Inn. There were mining works here from the 13th Century. By 1863 150 men were employed. The mine was abandoned by 1914 though the last tin was extracted from the "dumps" 1938/39. Substantial remains can still be seen, notably a wheel pit. To provide power for the mine, a leat was constructed to bring water from the East Dart. The leat starts near Sandy Hole pass at 625812, follows a long and winding route around Sittaford Tor and the Grey Wethers, through Fernworthy Forest, under the B3212 at Statts Bridge below the Warren House Inn, above the source of the Walla Brook and down to the mine. There, a little clapper spans a brook which eventually joins the West Webburn. The Vitifer mine was managed in the 19th Century by one Captain Paul/Paull/Palk – the names vary. He knew the richest tin lodes but didn't work them until the market went into recession – things don't change. He then persuaded the owners to sell him the mine, waited for fortunes to improve and became a rich man.

A small clapper over the stream at the Vitifer Mine, below the Warren House Inn. Start from the car-park 675811. On a sunny day it is a pleasant picnic site. It is a steep climb back.

Bog Asphodel
Narthecium ossifragum
The name reflects an old belief that it caused sheeps' bones to break. This is more likely due to calcium deficiency in moorland grazing. The plant was once used as saffron substitute. Some women used it as a hair dye.

WHEAL EMMA AND THE HOLNE MOOR LEATS

Wheal Emma was a copper mine whose remains are in Brook Wood, near Buckfastleigh. It was started in the early 1850s. 'Wheal,' incidentally, has nothing to do with 'Wheel'. Sometimes written in Cornish as 'Huel', it means 'a hole', which is basically what a mine is. Any mine in a watery area like Dartmoor has to have water pumped out all the time. To this end a 30ft wheel was first installed. This was powered by water taken from the nearby River Mardle. As the mine got deeper, this wheel proved not powerful enough, so a 46ft one was installed, leaving the old one to hoist ore up from the mine. Even this was not up to the job, so a 50ft one was ordered from a firm in Wales. Shipping proved impossible, so yet another (and cheaper) one was commissioned from Tavistock. The Mardle could not provide enough water to drive this so the leat was constructed in 1859 to bring water from the River Swincombe.

The leat starts where the Swincombe emerges from Foxtor Mires, 622710. A weir was built to divert water down the leat and a clapper bridge at the same site. There was some opposition to these works from the Duchy on behalf of farmers further downstream but, one way or another, these were overcome. The leat proceeds down the valley above the river, past Hexworthy, round Holne Moor where it flows parallel to Holne Moor leat and the Holne Town Gutter, round Venford reservoir and on round Holne Lee in square 6869 and eventually to a point about 680684, where its water was simply tipped down the hillside into the Mardle. Along its length the leat is crossed by numerous clappers, mostly now ruined, which allowed animals and farm vehicles access to grazing areas. Now, of course, the leat is all dry, but the clapper bridges remain and it makes a wonderful walk with some of the best views Dartmoor has to offer.

Heath Bedstraw
Galium saxatile
Perennial moorland plant, found all over UK, grows best on short, sheep-grazed grassy slopes. Slow growing, forms mats, flowers have sickly sweet scent. Food plant for Elephant Hawk Moth. Genus Galium includes Goose Grass.

129

Wheal Emma leat emerges from the mysterious and dangerous wastes of Foxtor Mires, inspiration for the Grimpen Mire in the Hound of the Baskervilles. There was a plan to make the wide basin into a reservoir, with a dam at this site but that plan was abandoned. As it is the vast quantity of peat and sphagnum moss form a natural reservoir to feed the Swincombe and then the Dart.

There are many varieties of heather, two of which are the main kinds found on Dartmoor.

Bell Heather
Erica cinerea
Its flowers, like little bells, are more colourful than the Ling and give the Moor its purple colour in late summer. Also found is the Cross-leaved Heath *Erica tetralix*.

130

The wild beauty of the R Swincombe. Wheal Emma leat on right. Far Hameldown

Leaving the Swincombe valley, the Wheal Emma leat turns eastwards round Down Ridge in sq 6571, being crossed all the way from its start by numerous clappers. The cart clapper below on the section above the river is typical. This section can be seen on the valley side in the main picture. There are a number of clappers, single slab and cart pattern, between the start of the leat and Hexworthy. This is a very wild part of the Moor. In the distance can be seen the dark shape of Hameldown, with Grimspound at the left and Widecombe to the right. At 663717 the sides of the leat are stone built and slots indicate that there was a sluice gate, see p135. Water was diverted down a pipe to an electricity generating station at Saddle Bridge. Nothing remains of that but there is room to park and round the bridge is a pleasant site. Power from here was taken uphill to Hensroost and Hooten Wheal mines. These produced a great deal of tin, first by open cast, later by deep mining, with water pumped out by their own wheel. But in 1920 a great storm demolished the aqueduct taking water to that and with it the poles carrying the power lines. The mine was flooded and that spelt the end of it. The remaining buildings were used as target practice during the 39-45 war.

Cart clapper on Wheal Emma leat : R Swincombe below right

Wheal Emma leat, down Swincombe, over Dart valley

At 642725 the R Swincombe is crossed by Fairy Bridge. This carries the track from Dartmeet via Hexworthy to Princetown. Part of this was intended by Thomas Tyrwitt to be developed into a road but was never finished. Close to the bridge are the ruins of John Bishop's house. He was a wall builder in the 19thC, whose works can still be seen around the Moor. Three systems can be seen here: stepping stones, piers on the banks and an approach ramp for a possible old clapper, and a modern wooden bridge. A stone bridge is a **clapper**, a wooden one is a **Clam**. On the skyline you can just make out a straight line of vegetation. That marks the course of Wheal Emma leat.

Holne Moor leat is also known as Hamlyn's leat. The Hamlyn family had a farm at Holne but left at the end of the 18th C and set up a woollen factory at Buckfast. Power for that was provided by a wheel driven by water from the Holy Brook but, as with Wheal Emma, more was needed, so Hamlyn's leat was built to add water to the brook, which it meets near Michelcombe 697689. After Venford reservoir, as the leats go round the slopes of Holne Lee, the map shows them crossing each other. This is done by reinforcing the bank of the leat to be crossed by wooden planks, with a small sluice gate inset which allows a ration of water through. The device is called a Launder. Such an arrangement can be seen where Holne town Gutter crosses Hamlyn's leat at 695698.

The sluice gate on Wheal Emma leat sent water down to drive the power station at Saddle Bridge

    Below Combestone, 670719, Emma is joined by the Holne Moor leat, still flowing, from its start on the O Brook. The two then run parallel round Venford reservoir, both dry, Holne Moor leat having taken a short cut across the valley in a pipe line, to re-emerge at a point on the eastern side. They are joined by the Holne Town Gutter, from Ringleshutes and still in use. At the head of the reservoir is a ruined clapper whose slabs are in the stream, replaced by a wooden footbridge, or Clam. There is ample parking at the dam and a pleasant walk round the reservoir.

    Though the bridge is ruined, its slabs are lying in the stream and it would be nice to think that DNPA might in time repair it as they have done with several others.

Passing Combestone Tor, Wheal Emma, dry and Holne Moor leat, flowing, run in parallel round Holne Moor. Combestone is said to be pronounced "Cumston" and so it may be but there is no need to write it that way, as some Moorland experts have done. From the ruined 3-slab clapper above, on a cold autumn evening, a view over the colourful Dart gorge. Below Combestone, a small stream goes down to the Dart. It is crossed by the little clapper, once broken, now restored and available for wheeled traffic. (max two wheels). It takes the track from Dartmeet to Venford.

A gate near Saddle Bridge 664719 gives access to land you are now allowed to cross. More or less straight uphill a little gate through the moor wall takes you onto the access land and to a track leading up to The Hensroost, scene of mining activity in years gone by. This cart clapper must have been very busy in its time. You can also get here by following the O Brook but it is a bit rough in parts. Having reached the Hensroost, a short walk further uphill takes you onto Skir Hill, and the great Girt, relic of old mining practices and the erosion caused, but now more gently covered in grass and trees. In this wildest part of the Moor you can see no signs of development in any direction.

Heath Milkwort
Polygala serpyllifolia
This pretty moorland plant has flowers of the most intense blue, with occasional pink or white varieties. It flowers from June to September, often seen with Tormentil. Polygala comes from the Greek, meaning much milk, and an old belief that cows grazing on the plant gave high yields of milk.

VENFORD RESERVOIR AND HOLNE MOOR

Take the western end of the reservoir as reference point at 686713. The dam carries the moorland road from Holne to Hexworthy. It was completed in 1907. The reservoir covers 33 acres and holds 198 million gallons. It was built to supply water to Paignton. By 1925 the supply was not sufficient so more water was taken from the river Swincombe. Water from the reservoir now supplies Widecombe, Ashburton and Brixham areas.

Holne Moor covers a wide area from the R Swincombe down to the Dart valley and the eastern slope of the south Moor. Archaeological evidence shows that there has been human activity for at least 4500 years, the busiest period being between 2000 – 1000 BCE. People lived in round houses and enclosed fields in patterns still visible. After 1066 medieval use continued much as before. Farmers built 'corn ditches' to separate the open Moor from cultivated land. The ditch had a shallow slope on the moorland side, down to a steep, reinforced face on the field side. Nowadays this would be called a 'Ha Ha'. Wheal Emma leat, Holne Moor or Hamlyn's leat and the Holne Town Gutter all come round Holne Moor in parallel, crossed by numerous clappers. From the eastern slope of the Venford valley you can see the traces of all three as they come round the reservoir.

A simple clapper on Wheal Emma leat overlooks Venford reservoir

From a small disused quarry a very handy car-park at 698699, a track leads up to the Ringleshutes mine area, 676699. Cart clappers carry the track across all three leats on the way up the hill. This gentleman was kind enough to point to another, smaller clapper which is now hidden by growths of bracken and gorse. In this area, Emma is dry, Holne Moor leat and Holne Town Gutter both flowing and in use. It is interesting to find the spot where they cross by means of a launder, at 695698.

How a flowing leat crosses another. Holne Moor, or Hamlyn's leat, coming round Holne Lee on its way to bolster the supply of water in the Holy Brook, is crossed by the Holne Town Gutter, coming straight down the slope. The sluice gate allows a ration of water into the village.

Off the Moor, eastern side, from Wheal Emma leat

Wheal Emma leat continues roughly south, round the head of the Holy Brook and eventually to the slope of the river Mardle, where it ends, the water being simply tipped down the hillside into the river. The combined waters were used to drive the wheels at the mine. On the way the leat is crossed by yet more clappers, mostly ruined, and the views over the Countryside east of the Moor are wonderful. Our final sight of Emma looks ahead to a line of beeches, actually an avenue through a deer farm. Those animals seen in the field are deer. We can now walk through the estate on the path where the beeches cast dramatic shadows over the track. Be very sure to close the gates at either end.

Sheep on Dartmoor. These are Scotch blackface sheep, the predominant breed on the Moor. They have been on the Moor since 1880, possibly introduced by Mr Gemell of Teignhead Farm. Their highland hardiness makes them ideally suited to the harsh conditions sometimes occurring. Dartmoor Whiteface and Greyface, a very long-woolled breed, may also be seen.

SOURCES AND RECOMMENDED READING

Dartmoor Walks into History — John Earle

Exploring Dartmoor - and "again" — Harry Starkey

Dartmoor 365 — John Hayward

Walking Dartmoor's ancient tracks
Walking the Dartmoor Waterways — Eric Hemery

On Dartmoor — Eden Phillpotts

The Dartmoor Worker
Ancient Stone Crosses of Dartmoor
The Land of Stream and Tor — William Crossing

The Book of Princetown — C Gardner-Thorpe

Dartmoor Sun — Jack Walker

A Perambulation of Dartmoor — Samuel Rowe

Dartmoor — R Hansford Worth

Follow the Leat — John Robins

The Clapper Bridge — Tom Greeves & Elizabeth Stanbrook

Most of these are available in County libraries. Some are out of print.

For Animals, Birds, Plants etc — Wikipedia

Copies of pictures of Moorland scenes can be obtained from the author, via email: regent47@virginmedia.com

Finally back to Teign e Ver where it all started and the classic clapper bridge.